D0617059

Sports

I Can Snowboard

By Edana Eckart

Children's Press®
A Division of Scholastic Inc.
New York / Toronto / London / Auckland / Sydney
Mexico City / New Delhi / Hong Kong
Danbury, Connecticut

Thanks to the Chill program. Chill is a non-profit learn-to-snowboard program for disadvantaged inner-city kids. For more information on this national intervention program, please contact jennd@burton.com.
Thanks to Burton Snowboard Company

Photo Credits: Cover and all photos by Maura B. McConnell
Contributing Editor: Jennifer Silate
Book Design: Mindy Liu

Library of Congress Cataloging-in-Publication Data

Eckart, Edana.
  I can snowboard / by Edana Eckart.
  p. cm. — (Sports)
  Summary: When a young boy goes snowboarding, he shows how to slide down a hill properly and safely.
  Includes bibliographical references (p.) and index.
  ISBN 0-516-24281-4 (lib. bdg.) — ISBN 0-516-24373-X (pbk.)
  1. Snowboarding--Juvenile literature. [1. Snowboarding.] I. Title.

GV857.S57 E37 2003
796.9--dc21   2002007007

Contents

My name is Tony.

Today, I am going
to **snowboard**.

4

5

I put on my **helmet**.

It will keep my head safe if I fall.

I also wear **goggles**.

They will help to keep
the snow out of my eyes.

9

I wear special **boots** to snowboard.

Each boot fits onto the snowboard.

Now, the snowboard will stay on my feet.

11

I stand up on
my snowboard.

I am **careful** not to fall.

13

I **lean** forward.

My snowboard moves
on the snow.

15

I lean back to turn.

17

I go down the hill.

I am careful not to hit anyone else.

19

I made it to the bottom of the hill.

Snowboarding is fun!

21

New Words

boots (**boots**) heavy shoes that cover your ankles
and sometimes part of your legs

careful (**kair**-fuhl) to pay close attention when
doing something

goggles (**gog**-uhlz) special glasses that fit tightly
around your eyes to protect them

helmet (**hel**-mit) a hard hat that protects your head
during sports

lean (**leen**) to bend toward or over something

snowboard (**snoh**-bord) a flat piece of wood or
other material that is fastened to boots; to ride
on a snowboard

To Find Out More

Books
Beginning Snowboarding
by Julie Jensen
Lerner Publishing Group

Snowboarding
by Bob Italia
ABDO Publishing

Web Site
CBC 4 Kids: Snowboarding
http://www.cbc4kids.cbc.ca/general/whats-new/sport-of-the-month/
    january99/default.html
This Web site has a lot of information, plus tips for snowboarding.

Index

boot, 10

goggles, 8

helmet, 6
hill, 18, 20

lean, 14, 16

snow, 8, 14
snowboard, 4, 10

About the Author
Edana Eckart has written several children's books. She enjoys bike riding with her family.

Reading Consultants
Kris Flynn, Coordinator, Small School District Literacy, The San Diego County Office of Education

Shelly Forys, Certified Reading Recovery Specialist, W.J. Zahnow Elementary School, Waterloo, IL

Sue McAdams, Former President of the North Texas Reading Council of the IRA, and Early Literacy Consultant, Dallas, TX